Jesse James

A Captivating Guide to a Wild West Outlaw Who Robbed Trains, Banks, and Stagecoaches across the Midwestern United States

Free Bonus from Captivating History (Available for a Limited time)

Hi History Lovers!

Now you have a chance to join our exclusive history list so you can get your first history ebook for free as well as discounts and a potential to get more history books for free! Simply visit the link below to join.

Captivatinghistory.com/ebook

Also, make sure to follow us on Facebook, Twitter and Youtube by searching for Captivating History.

Contents

Introduction

In the minds of many Americans, the name of Jesse James and the Wild West are practically synonymous. The bank robberies, with bullets flying from one side to the other of a dusty little town of the American frontier; the daring train robberies, with locomotives being chased by horses and forced to make a halt only to be boarded by gentlemanly bandits; the spectacular escapes of horse riders camouflaged by long coats, firing two revolvers, one in each hand. All of these are episodes that correspond to the life of Jesse James, that notable son of Missouri. In this sense, he is a vital and representative part of American history and life.

Jesse James was a robber, a murderer, and a notorious outlaw, who carried as many weapons as he could. He could shoot with both hands while he held the reins of his horse in his teeth. He was an extremely popular man in his day, a phenomenon that he readily accepted because he was a person who craved attention. He supposedly gave part of his booty to the poor, although no evidence of this can be found except in folklore.

Frontiersmen like James, who has been regarded as a monster, a vigilante, a modern Robin Hood, and as the last rebel of the Civil War, have a special appeal in the American imagination. Had he been born a century later, we would probably know him with a different name, perhaps as one of the FBI's Most Wanted; his face would possibly appear on television next to the word "terrorist" because he chose targets with political statements in mind.

It is true that he was in it for the money, but the robberies of banks, trains, and other institutions had a political edge, and his deeds attracted the sympathy of many locals, who resented the domination of big business. The newspapers, especially in the editorials of his friend John Newman Edwards, glorified his deeds for a political purpose. To some, Jesse James was the voice of those who had been defeated in the Civil War, the necessary symbol of resistance and nonconformity, and the face of the "Lost Cause," which embodied the anger of the South. Journalist John Newman Edwards essentially created a Robin Hood out of a merciless robber.

Even in our time, when there is more information than in the days when Jesse James's adventures were spread by word of mouth, many still see him as more than a bandit. Perhaps the fascination with him derives from the fact that he was a bank and train robber. But he is also seen as a romantic figure from the Wild West, as someone who rebelled against larger, overwhelming forces, forces that still makes us feel insignificant and expendable today. Jesse challenged them all and scoffed at them while doing so.

There is, without a doubt, more than one way to see Jesse James. We just have to remember the words of late historian William A. Settle: "Badman or Robin Hood, take your choice! Whichever form of the legend you please, both are based in fact."

Chapter One – A Boy Named Jesse

"We called him outlaw, and he was, but Fate made him so."

–John Newman Edwards

Jesse James was born in 1847 to a family on the American frontier. His parents were named Robert Sallee James and Zerelda. They were originally a couple from Kentucky who moved to Clay County, Missouri, five years before Jesse's birth. His father was a Baptist minister and a part of the so-called Second Great Awakening, a Protestant revival that swept the United States in the mid-1800s. His mother, Zerelda, was a tall, opinionated, and dominating woman. The couple met at a religious gathering and got married when she was only seventeen years old. They soon moved to the small town of Kearney in Clay County, Missouri, where they settled with the help of relatives. Jesse's father founded the Baptist temples of New Hope and Providence there.

The couple's first child was named Frank, who was followed by another boy named Robert, who died at a young age. Jesse Woodson James came next. Although he was too young to be fully aware of what he was seeing, in his early years, he must have witnessed his father fervently preaching from the pulpit of his small Baptist temple or seen members of his congregation experience states of fervor, piety, and even mass hysteria at camp meetings. On one occasion, Jesse's father baptized sixty-four people in the river in a single day, without leaving the water once. This seems like an unlikely background for one of the most legendary bandits in the United States. The abilities of Robert James as a preacher must have been extraordinary, for, in a short time, he managed to convert the small log cabin that he inherited into a respectable temple, and he vastly increased the number of the faithful who attended his sermons.

Camp meetings were a religious phenomenon suited to the rural setting of frontier towns. Since the population density was low, this meant there were fewer churches, and people traveled long distances to have religious experiences at these meetings, which could last from four to seven days. The people sang hymns and listened to itinerant preachers of austere morals. In those places, some of the great religious hymns that persist to this day were created, in some cases spontaneously.

In 1847, the year Jesse was born, the war between Mexico and the United States came to an end. As a result of the conflict, the northern part of Mexico was absorbed by the United States as spoils of war. This fact had consequences for the James family. Just a year after the peace agreement, in which California became part of the American Union, the first reports of gold began to arrive. A real fever exploded amongst the Americans to go and get some of those riches. People heard the news of huge finds, of tales that one could find more gold than the fruit of a whole year's labor on a farm in a single day. Pastor James, even though his priority was to save souls, could not avoid temptation and left in 1851 for the West, although he also supposedly wanted to preach to the prospectors.

Four-year-old Jesse held onto his father's leg, begging him not to leave. Perhaps this was a presage for Zerelda, who knew that day that she would never see her husband again. However, the pastor expected to get rich and return with enough money for his family. Sadly,

Zerelda's premonition would come true. Instead of seeing her man return laden with gold, Zerelda opened the door to strange, grave-faced men, who broke the news that her husband had died of cholera in the Wild West. Jesse's father had not survived more than one month in California.

For the family, this was the beginning of great difficulties, especially since, according to the legislation of the time, the widow did not automatically inherit the farm. The creditors threw themselves on her, expecting to collect the debt by auctioning off her properties. The three small children went to live with relatives. After a while, in 1852, Zerelda married again to a man named Benjamin Simms. This marriage was not lucky either, as the man also died, leaving Zerelda widowed a second time. Remembered as a tall, strong-willed woman who was resistant to adversity, Zerelda was unwilling to see her three young children—Frank, James, and baby Susan—starve to death. She married a third time, this time to a man younger than her. His name was Dr. Reuben Samuels, and Zerelda managed to convince him to give up medicine and dedicate himself to farm work. The small property finally began to flourish again. The family hired temporary workers, but the farm prospered thanks to the work of seven black slaves that they owned. Jesse and his brother James attended school when they could, but they spent most of their time working on the farm, riding horses, and learning to shoot a gun.

According to a writer of the time, young Jesse had a face as smooth and as innocent as the face of a schoolgirl, with piercing blue eyes and a delicate figure. He and his brother Frank had everything to live a good life. Their lives in rural Missouri were pleasant and tranquil, but that was about to change.

The Civil War

After swallowing half of Mexico, the United States almost doubled in size, but indigestion followed soon after. The 1850s were marked by division over the issue of slavery. Both Missouri and the adjacent territories of Kansas and Nebraska were being settled by people who were both for and against slavery. The topic divided families and neighbors.

Tempers grew hot, and violence arose between both sides, first verbal, then physical. The region became a red-hot war zone. Many locals formed guerrilla bands to attack anti-slavery towns in neighboring Kansas. Missouri was flooded with spies, guerrillas, and militias who were for and against secession. These armed men not only fought among themselves, but they also harassed and killed civilians.

In 1861, the Civil War began in the United States, whose fire was fueled by the social division around slavery. The issue disunited Missourians too. Although the state remained loyal to the Union, many families wanted to belong to the South, so they formed resistance groups called bushwhackers. In 1861, eighteen-year-old Frank James, Jesse's older brother, went to fight with the Missouri State Guard. Jesse was fifteen and still too young to fight with the State Guard or the bushwhackers, who had no formal connection with the Confederate Army but were still doing their best to create chaos among the Union ranks.

Jesse's mother had a clear pro-slavery stance. The abolitionists detested her because she was very vocal about her sympathies for the Southern cause and because of her strong and determined personality that agitated many People. Zerelda and Dr. Samuels also had a financial motive. The operation of their farm depended on the slaves. Besides, many slaveholders had formed strong bonds with their slaves, which they considered to be almost as strong as family ties. Of course, they could not understand that in order for the bond to be genuine, it had to be accepted by both sides.

Zerelda railed against the Union, and she served as a spy for the rebels and fed the guerrillas, of which her eldest son Frank was a militant. The guerrillas robbed civilians and killed their war prisoners. One day in June 1863, a party of armed men belonging to the Union arrived at the farm of Dr. Samuels and his wife, Zerelda. They entered violently, demanding the woman tell them the whereabouts of William Quantrill, who was the leader of the guerilla forces in Missouri.

Sixteen-year-old Jesse James was plowing with his stepfather when the gunmen broke in. They violently dragged Dr. Samuels to a tree on the property. After pulling out a rope, they hung the doctor from one of the branches until he was almost dead. They brought him down, and after reviving him, they demanded that he reveal Quantrill's whereabouts, but the doctor swore that he did not know. Unconvinced by the answer, they hung him again, while others dragged young Jesse through the tobacco fields and whipped him with a rope before forcing him to watch his stepfather being hanged. They also pointed a gun at his mother, who was pregnant at the time. The men threatened to kill the doctor if his wife did not say what she knew. "What I know, I will die knowing" was the answer that Zerelda's grandson recorded in his memoirs, which he wrote when Zerelda was still living. Then Zerelda asked the men what they intended to do with her husband. "We're going to kill him and let the hogs eat him," they told her. Zerelda then heard several gunshots.

Zerelda thought she had become a widow again, but the men had only taken Dr. Samuels away. Under brutal pressure, he finally revealed what the soldiers wanted to know. It was that or lose his life. The mistreated Jesse went to his mother and showed her the stripes on his back. Zerelda wept at the sight of the bruises, but her son told her she shouldn't cry. "Ma, don't you cry. I'll not stand this again." He then expressed his resolution to join Quantrill and his guerrilla. "But they have stolen all the horses, and you have no money," said his mother. In the spring of 1864, Jesse parted with the guerrilla in a unit led by one of Quantrill's men, "Bloody" Bill Anderson, who was one of the fiercest men in one of the bloodiest wars on the continent.

* * *

Being part of "Bloody" Bill Anderson's gang surely had a crushing effect on an angry and hurt young man like Jesse. William Anderson, a man that looked like a pirate, had also seen his father mistreated and murdered by a judge. "Bloody" Bill Anderson killed his father's assassin and became a fugitive, storming the roads. Two of his sisters died while under arrest, and Bill vowed revenge. His methods were inhuman. He never took prisoners, and he let his men mutilate and behead their victims to such an extent that many historians consider him a psychopathic and sadistic murderer. The adolescent Jesse James participated in the massacres, and the guerrillas also looted towns, stole liquor, and executed unarmed Union soldiers. Sometimes they even scalped them—such was the brutality of the war on the frontier. Jesse also learned how to ride a horse, as well as how to use both hands to shoot while controlling his mount by holding the reins with his teeth. He also earned the nickname "Dingus" among his fellow guerrillas, supposedly because that was what he furiously yelled when he accidentally blew off a piece of his finger from his left hand.

On July 10th, 1864, the guerrillas raided the city of Platte City, Missouri. Jesse was among the forty men who entered the city. The town surrendered without a fight, and the men defending it took the oath to serve the Confederacy. Two days later, the *New York Times* reported, "All of the arms were brought out and turned over to the raiders. With scarcely an exception, they were welcomed with open arms; a rebel flag was hoisted; the women of the place, old and young, immediately set to work making rebel flags as emblems for their horses and badges to be worn in their hats." This was not a famous battle of the Civil War or a heinous date remembering a massacre, but according to some sources, it was here in Platte City, on this date, that sixteen-year-old Jesse James had his most famous picture taken. The image shows the young teenager in a typical bushwhacker shirt, looking like a juvenile pirate, with a long revolver in his hand.

The Carnage of Centralia

In September of that year, pro-Confederate fighters looted the small town of Centralia, burned the railroad station, and then brutally executed twenty-four Union soldiers who had just arrived on the train.

The soldiers were young, unprepared, and unarmed. The guerrillas pulled them off the wagons, stripped them naked to keep their uniforms as disguises, then shot them point-blank one by one. The guerrillas proceeded to mutilate the bodies and scalp some of them. It was one of the bloodiest acts of the Civil War, and Jesse was part of it. Some horrified civilians protested only to get killed too. According to Frank James, Jesse killed his first man here, a man named Major Johnston. It would be the first in a long list.

Seeking to punish the guilty, a task force led by Major Andrew B. E. Johnston went with 150 men after them. But the decision was catastrophic. A small detachment of guerrillas ambushed them at the top of a hill. The enemy approached them from all sides and massacred every man. Some of them begged for mercy only to be tortured until death. Then, completely mad with the smell of blood, the bushwhackers beheaded every soldier that lay on the hill. When the Union troops arrived at the site, they were beyond words at the sight of the mutilated bodies. Scattered decapitated heads greeted the incoming soldiers with horrified expressions, and some heads even had their own private parts stuck in their mouths. One can only wonder what doing and seeing this did to the psyche of the young Missourian. Certainly, a normal life was out of the question for any of the men from that day on.

Chapter Two – Back Home

"Proscribed, hunted, shot, driven away from among his people, a price put upon his head—what else could the man do, with such a nature, except what he did do? He had to live. It was his country. The graves of his kindred were there. He refused to be banished from his birthright, and when he was hunted, he turned savagely about and hunted his hunters."

–John N. Edwards

In 1865, with the triumph of the Union, the Civil War came to an end. More than 600,000 people perished, but in many places like Missouri, no one believed that the war was really over. The resentment and violence did not end overnight. Although the Confederate Army surrendered, many bushwhackers were still active in the field, wishing for revenge. For the United States, it would be the beginning of a long road to reconciliation, and it would not be an easy one.

Jesse had escaped to Texas with seventy other bushwhackers. When he learned that the defeated Southern soldiers were allowed to return to their homes and farms, he went back to Missouri in June of that year. In July, his brother Frank voluntarily surrendered to the Union. Their mother, Zerelda, had been arrested during that difficult period in which the animosity between factions was still red-hot. When Jesse James's gang arrived in Missouri and found out about General Robert E. Lee's surrender, they said it was surely a Yankee lie. Along the way, they committed atrocities disguised as Union soldiers. They looted towns, and James even cold-bloodedly murdered the Kingsville postmaster.

However, the truth is that they were debating between giving up, accepting the offer to return home in peace, or continuing to terrorize and fight. More and more rebels were embracing the amnesty and taking the oath of allegiance to the Union, swearing that they would not commit acts of rebellion so they could go back to their families. But many of them were also penniless, their property mortgaged.

As Jesse and other men approached Lexington, a squad of cavalrymen opened fire on them. The order of events in this unfortunate event is unclear. According to one version, the men approached in peace, waving a white flag, and the Union soldiers fired when they saw them because they knew they were former guerrillas. According to a witness that recalled the scene twenty years later, the Union soldiers had only approached the gang to escort them, but the guerrillas' nerves wavered, causing some to flee. This led an inexperienced soldier to open fire amid the confusion. James himself later narrated that he was going to Lexington to take the amnesty. Whatever it was, the moment was decisive for the genesis of the bandit.

In the skirmish, a projectile penetrated Jesse's chest and became lodged in his lung. While he was being pursued by two men on horseback, he turned to kill one of the horses and barely escaped into the woods, where he lay by the water all night. The next day, a farmer found him and dragged him to his house.

Jesse could barely walk, but with the help of one of his former comrades, he managed to reach a hotel room, where they took the oath of allegiance to the Union and surrendered. But the danger of death had not passed, as the bullet was still in his lung. Jesse made it to Nebraska, where his mother had moved. He was so close to death that Zerelda would put her ear to his chest just to see if his heart was still beating. The remainder of his convalescence was spent at his uncle John Mimms's home in the village of Harlem, where his cousin Zerelda (who was named after his mother) nursed him. The cousins fell in love. "Ma, I am going to marry Zee," he told Zerelda when he recovered. Jesse got baptized and joined the Baptist church. But holiness and marriage weren't really in his plans.

The Clay County Savings Bank

The bullet stayed in Jesse's lung his entire life, but the ex-combatant recovered. As soon as he was healed, he joined a new group of former guerrillas. But the raison d'être of the bushwhackers had vanished. As in many other wars in other countries, peace did not come without difficulties. The most pressing question was what would happen to the hordes of armed, angry young men like Frank and Jesse. All they knew was how to shoot a gun, fight, and lead desperate lives. The brothers would not accept defeat and go back to the simple farming life.

Jesse joined Archie Clement's gang—a pro-Confederate ex-guerrilla remembered for his cruelty—with the idea of robbing banks. Banks weren't simply the places where people saved their money. Many saw them as Northern instruments of control, as places that mortgaged the properties of farmers who could not pay their interest. In other words, they were instruments of oppression. The Clay County Bank, which was located where many ex-guerrillas like Jesse James lived, was probably the first daylight bank robbery in the United States, a scene that would become common in the years to come.

February 13th, 1866, seemed like a normal day inside the Clay County Savings Bank. At two o'clock in the afternoon, the main teller, a man named Bird, was working when two men approached the counter, put a ten-dollar bill on the desk, and asked him to change it for them. Bird's son approached to assist the strangers when he realized they had guns. One of them jumped over the counter, threatened the young man, and ordered him to go to the vault and put the money inside a cotton sack. The young Bird began to fill the sack with bags of gold coins, while another bandit threatened his father with a revolver.

When the cashier's son finished, Mr. Bird was taken inside the vault. The two bandits left the bank to meet the rest of the gang. In a few seconds, they had managed to seize almost $60,000—nearly a million dollars in today's money. At that moment, Bird appeared, as the thieves had forgotten to close the door to the vault. The exasperated cashier began to shout that the bank had been robbed. A dozen outlaws fled down the street, firing their pistols into the air, while a party was organized to follow them. Within days, posters were hung on the street, offering a reward. It has not been possible to establish with absolute certainty that Frank and Jesse James were among the dozen men who galloped down the street, shooting at the bewildered inhabitants of Liberty. However, it is a fact that they belonged to the former men of "Bloody" Bill Anderson, who had been captured and executed by the commander of the Union, Samuel P. Cox, in 1864.

At the end of 1866, the gang entered another bank in Lexington, Missouri. They approached the teller, who managed to close the vault just in time, and the bandits left the town empty-handed. They had much greater luck in the spectacular December robbery in Richmond, Missouri. The clan gathered outside the Hughes & Mason Bank, but the neighbors became suspicious when two of the strangers stepped inside while the others waited outside. The inhabitants of Richmond approached the building, and after noticing that the men were hostile, they unleashed a shower of bullets on the bandits, who escaped after taking the money. The outlaws shot at the people as they tried to leave the town, killing the mayor of Richmond. They headed for the Crooked River, but a party of fifteen men was on their heels, firing their guns. So, Jesse and his band turned and shot their horses. They finally split up and escaped. In the following weeks, the indignant people of Richmond lynched several people that looked suspicious to them. After all, at a time when there were no insurance or bank bailouts, they knew that the thugs had taken their savings for good.

Jesse James Becomes (In)Famous

Jesse James's gang began to set their sights beyond Missouri. Knowing that the alerted residents of their home state might be prepared to confront them in the event of another robbery, they decided to strike the next blow in Kentucky. There, they met an even more surprising reaction. In March 1868, brothers Frank and Jesse left the small town's hotel with at least five other bank robbers, after having planned the details of the job and buying horses and weapons in Russellville. One of them pretended to be a cattle buyer and went to check the bank before the big day. When the hour came, two other men did the usual trick. One entered the building, went to the counter, and asked the teller to change a bill for him. After losing his patience, the outlaw planted the mouth of his revolver on the head of the cashier, Nimrod Long, who ran bravely to the back door and began calling for help.

Several armed people rushed to defend the bank where their modest savings were deposited. Many came, some with buckets of water, as they thought the building was on fire. The James brothers and their henchmen fled with more than $12,000. The bank owner decided to hire a detective to hunt down the fugitives. Several of the robbers fell into the hands of the law. The James brothers, possibly feeling they should keep a low profile for a while, disappeared for a few months. Historians have speculated what became of Jesse for most of 1868 and 1869. Some believe that he was in New York, and others place him in California as a cowboy, working on his uncle's farm.

Jesse returned in a brutal way before the end of 1869 to launch his first solo robbery, accompanied by his brother Frank. At noon on December 7th, 1869, he got off his horse and headed inside the

Daviess County Savings Association in Gallatin, Missouri, while his older brother waited outside. He headed to the back of the bank, where the teller was writing at his desk. The bandit repeated the trick: he produced a $100 note and asked it to be changed. As the cashier examined the paper to determine its value, Jesse pulled a huge revolver from his clothes and pronounced the death sentence of the terrified clerk. "Cox, this is my revenge." Then he shot him point-blank. Jesse was sure he had killed Major Samuel P. Cox, who was responsible for the death of "Bloody" Bill Anderson, whom Jesse considered a brother. Behind him, a lawyer, who had his office on the bank's premises, panicked and ran toward the exit. Reacting quickly, the bandit shot him twice. Before escaping, Jesse grabbed a suitcase from the bank.

The brothers had just left the bank when they heard the first shots behind them. The neighbors were ready to strike back. Jesse's horse jerked, and he fell from his saddle. He was dragged for several feet until he released his boot from the stirrup. When an alarmed Frank spotted him on the ground, he turned around and hoisted him onto his mount. They fled together, with the inhabitants of Daviess almost on their heels. When the brothers found Honey Creek and knew their tracks had been lost, and they opened the briefcase. There was not a dollar there—just worthless papers. But for Jesse, it had been a successful journey because he had killed Samuel P. Cox. He would be greatly surprised later when he found out that Cox was still alive and that the poor teller had been the owner and sole employee of the bank.

The news spread like wildfire. Jesse James started to become a well-known figure, feared by some, considered to be a brave and exciting fellow to others—thus began his curious transformation into a kind of folk hero. Anecdotes about his misdeeds when he stole people's savings circulated by word of mouth. In 1871, after convincing the cashier of the bank in Croydon, Iowa, to give him all the money in the safe, the fleeing gang approached a political rally that was taking place in the yard of the local Methodist church, where a politician was giving a speech to the community. According to some testimonies, Jesse interrupted the attorney, Henry Clay Dean, and said that he needed to say something important. The speaker, a little impatient, asked him what it was. "Well, sir," said Jesse, "I reckon it's important enough. The fact is, Mr. Dean, some fellows have been over to the bank and tied up the cashier, and if you all ain't too busy you might ride over and untie him. I've got to be going." By the time the people reached the door of Ocobock Brothers Bank, the band was far from Croydon.

The gang members weren't always the same, especially since several months passed between the robberies. Some were arrested, others were killed, and some took advantage of the amnesty that the government offered them. Jesse established himself as the natural leader of the gang, which included the core members of Frank and the Younger brothers—Cole, Jim, John, and Bob.

Chapter Three – An Unlikely Ally

One might think the notorious outlaw savored his misdeeds because Jesse wrote elegant letters about his robberies to newspapers, in which some of them he claimed his innocence. After the unfortunate incident in Gallatin, where he confused and murdered the cashier, he wrote a letter to a Kansas City newspaper addressed to the governor, declaring to be guiltless and saying that he was certain that if he appeared in public, he would not have a fair trial. "I well know if I was to submit to an arrest, that I would be mobbed and hanged without a trial."

Although Jesse was a good reader, those well-written letters he sent to newspapers were not completely the product of his own mind. They were most certainly heavily edited or even wholly written by a helping hand, an unlikely ally, the aforementioned newspaper editor named John Newman Edwards, a former Confederate major and journalist with whom the highwayman befriended around this time.

John N. Edwards was born in Virginia, and he was eight years older than Jesse. He was a composer, but he had also worked as a printer and had been in the Civil War on the side of the Confederacy. He later settled in Missouri, where he became a newspaper editor and an advocate for the so-called "Lost Cause." Edwards had a strange fascination about Jesse, one that bordered on enthusiasm and adoration. In Jesse, Edwards saw a symbol of the unconformity of the defeated. He also saw the opportunity to have a symbol for the South, an anti-hero. With this new symbol, Edwards hoped to achieve what the Confederates had not been able to accomplish with arms: to keep the rebellion alive. Therefore, Edwards served as a sort of PR man to the James brothers and their gang. "They come and go as silently as the leaves fall," he wrote. "They never boast. They have many names and many disguises. They speak low, are polite, deferential and accommodating. They do not kill save in stubborn self-defense. They have nothing in common with a murderer. They hate the highwayman and the coward. They are outlaws, but they are not criminals, no matter what prejudiced public opinion may declare."

Through his editorials, Edwards presented James as a good man who was simply rebelling against the big capitalists who had the working families of the South under their thumbs. Jesse James and his gang were waging war against the greed of the North, which was represented by the banks. "Fate made him so," Edwards wrote. He reported that Jesse wouldn't take money from ex-Confederate soldiers, nor from honest, working men. While some newspapers wrote about the robberies with disgust and outrageous adjectives, Edwards penned his articles as if he were reviewing an entertaining Wild West film. For example, when Jesse and his brother stormed the box office of the Industrial Exposition in Kansas City, Edwards wrote in the *Kansas City Times*, "It was a deed so high-handed, so diabolically daring and so utterly in contempt of fear that we are bound to admire go and revere its perpetrators for the very enormity of their outlawry." Thus, Jesse was, in Edwards's eyes, a working-class hero, a maverick rebel who enjoyed making the powerful mad. "With them, booty is but the second thought; the wild drama of the adventure first."

In the rural South, the bankers and the railroads were especially hated. The bankers confiscated the land of the peasants when they defaulted on their payments, and the railroads seized rich land for nothing to lay tracks. On top of everything, the government had raised taxes to finance the construction of more railroads. Knowing that a man from the South was kicking the giants—someone who, like them, had grown up on a farm—delighted ordinary people, even if they did not receive a part of the loot. Through his editorials, Edwards cultivated this image to perfection. "The war made them desperate guerrillas...they were men who could not be bullied who were too intrepid to be tyrannized...They were hunted, and they were human. They replied to proscription by defiance, ambushment by ambushment, musket shot by pistol shot, night attack by counter-attack, charge by counter-charge, and so will they do, desperately and with splendid heroism, until the end."

Jesse was self-conscious about his public image, and he liked to cultivate it. On one occasion, for example, during a coach robbery, Jesse announced that he would inspect the hands of all passengers. If anyone had hard and callused hands, a sign that they were working men, he would respect them and leave their items alone. According to him, he also refrained from robbing ex-Confederate soldiers. On another occasion, when he was leaving a bank, he left a letter with a description of the events and a blank line for the cashier to fill in with the total amount stolen by the gang. The letter was possibly written by Edwards. Someone with Jesse's precarious formal education could hardly have written, "We are not thieves, we are bold robbers. I am proud of the name, for Alexander the Great was a bold robber, and Julius Caesar, and Napoleon Bonaparte."

In 1877, Edwards published his controversial book, *Noted guerrillas, Or, The warfare of the Border*, where he recounted the lives of former Confederates turned bandits as if they were heroes. The book justified the misdeeds of people like Quantrill, Bill Anderson, and, of course, brothers Frank and Jesse, about whom he said, "Since 1865 it has been pretty much one eternal ambush for these two men, one unbroken and eternal hunt twelve years long...By some intelligent people they are regarded as myths; by others as in league with the devil. They are neither, but they are uncommon men. Neither touches whiskey. Neither travels twice the same road."

But how much of the brothers' activity was motivated by greed, and how much was political spectacle? Although they never put their activism or supposed chivalry above monetary interest, the truth is that Jesse James became aware of his public persona and used it to promote the "Lost Cause." After yet another bank break-in but before making himself scarce, he shot into the air, shouting hurrahs for former Confederate generals.

A "Mobile Bank"

So, while Edwards was dedicated to turning Jesse into a mythical figure, a kind of lovable anti-hero, Jesse was busy diversifying his criminal activities. With each new job, Jesse and his brother became more ambitious and confident, thanks to the support of the people. If only he could find banks far enough from the town's main street so as not to be seen and hunted by neighbors, a bank far from lawmen. It would be even better if that bank went away after they robbed it and to walk off with more than the meager savings of villagers. As incredible as it may seem, there were vaults with those characteristics, a vault that was more profitable, safer for the gang, and certainly more exciting: trains.

During those years, there had been an expansion in the construction of railways. For many in the South and frontier towns, the trains were a symbol of the economic and political dominance of the North and corporations affiliated to the Republican Party. Taxes had been increased for their construction. Besides, rail lines transported much larger riches than what modest banks could hold in their safes. In 1848, gold had been discovered in California, and large shipments were carried from the West to safe vaults on the East Coast. Besides, as T. J. Stiles wrote, "all year long, physical stocks of money moved toward New York, to return in the fall to the spawning grounds in the countryside. And it all went by rail." In other words, trains were the ideal victims.

The robbery of the Chicago, Rock Island and Pacific Railroad in July 1873 was spectacular; it produced headlines across the country, and the size of the felony left more than one commentator speechless. Although railroad robberies had occurred before, this was the first armed occupation of a train at the hands of a hostile party. The site was carefully chosen. The gang decided to strike a section of the track where the tracks curved, meaning the train had to reduce its speed. It was far from any town and near a bridge; it was the ideal place to attack and disappear in less than fifteen minutes. The band waited in hiding, about fifty feet from the track. When they heard the sound of the locomotive, they bent the rails out of place with a cord. The engine driver watched the intrusion and desperately tried to stop the vehicle without success. The train passed over the wrecked track, and the locomotive toppled over, although the rest of the train was unharmed. The assailants opened fire on any window where a face appeared.

One of the assailants boarded the second wagon, where the transcontinental express shipment and some gold was supposedly stored. Jesse approached the company employee guarding the shipment and took off his mask. Later, witnesses reported, "The man who seemed to be the leader...light hair, blue eyes, heavy sandy whiskers, broad shoulders and a straight, tolerably short nose, a little turned up; a tolerably high, broad forehead, intelligent looking, looked like a tolerably well educated man and did not look like a working man." That was, without a doubt, the legendary Jesse James. He demanded the man to open the safe or else. Meanwhile, in the passenger cars, other bandits walked through the corridors, looking at the terrified faces of the gentlemen and hearing the sobs of the women. "We're none of your petty thieves; we're bold robbers," they said, with their guns in the air. "We're robbing the rich for the poor.

We don't want to hurt you; we're going through the express car."
They wore masks like the Ku-Klux Klan. Both their speech and the
masks were clear political statements. Other sources claim that the
men actually robbed the passengers, probably after they learned there
was no gold in the safe. With their task done, the men climbed onto
their horses and fled with less than $3,000 and no gold, far less than
they expected. The next day, they would learn from the newspapers
that the gold shipment they had hoped to steal had been shipped the
night before.

It was the first train robbery west of the Mississippi, and it basically
amounted to a military occupation of the vehicle. Suddenly, James
became a national figure; some saw him as a dangerous thug, while
others realized he was an improbable hero that capitalized on
"Missouri's rage against the railroads." If anything, the nation was
flabbergasted. The event made headlines across the United States. A
$5,000 reward was offered by the railroad company, but the
"gentlemanly" robbers escaped unharmed. To hunt them down, the
company hired the Pinkerton National Detective Agency of Chicago.
The agency had been founded in 1850 by a Scottish spy named Allan
Pinkerton. Pinkerton proved his credentials when he discovered a
plot to assassinate President Abraham Lincoln. When the famous
agency was hired in 1874 to hunt down the James and Younger
brothers, its founder would take that mission as a personal matter.

Chapter Four – Northfield: A Watershed

"They wouldn't let me stay at home, so what else can I do?"

—Jesse James, on his life as a bandit after the Civil War

The brothers disappeared in the months that followed the famous train robbery. They were fed and protected by locals who thought they were still championing the cause of the South. During these months, Jesse's admirer, journalist John Newman Edwards, perfected Jesse's larger than life figure and turned him into almost a hero.

In April 1874, Jesse married his long-time girlfriend and first cousin Zee James after ten years of romance. The ceremony was at the house of Zee's sister, and her uncle, a Methodist minister, presided. The wedding was almost perfect, except for a cop alarm in the middle of the ceremony. All the guests ran for cover, and after realizing the cops weren't actually there, the wedding resumed. Edwards ran a humorous editorial: "CAPTURED! The Celebrated Jesse W. James Taken at Last. His Captor a Woman, Young, Accomplished, and Beautiful." The couple apparently honeymooned in Texas at the beaches of Galveston, where Jesse might have been spotted by a reporter of the *St. Louis Dispatch*, as he claimed to have seen the famous outlaw. Always with work in mind, Jesse apparently robbed a few stagecoaches during the honeymoon. However, as with many other things about Jesse, it's sometimes hard to tell fact from legend.

A year later, the couple saw the birth of their first son, Jesse Edward. There would be no peace for their marriage, as Pinkerton continued to hunt Jesse, his most coveted prey, in inept and dirty ways. A few months after the wedding, the detectives of the agency, called the Pinkertons, thought they could hunt him down at his house, and to that end, they surrounded Dr. Samuels's farm. During the night, they decided to set fire to the building with an artifact, which they threw through the window. This item was an "iron ball surrounded by kerosene-soaked cotton." Unfortunately, the device ended up in the family's chimney, where it exploded. The metal fragments killed Jesse's half-brother, a son of Samuels, and shattered his mother's arm. The agents panicked and escaped. The press was sympathetic to the brothers and attacked the Pinkertons mercilessly. Indignant over the events that had transpired, Jesse made a vow to go after the main detective and take revenge. According to Jesse himself, he found Allan Pinkerton in Chicago and had many chances to kill him, but he ended up going back to Missouri with his thirst for vengeance unquenched. "I had a dozen chances to kill him when he didn't know it. It wouldn't do me no good if I couldn't tell him about it before he died. I want him to know who did it."

A Disaster in Northfield

Despite the pleas of his wife, Jesse continued his career as a bandit with even more determination. In July 1876, he robbed another train, where a traveling minister made passengers sing religious hymns while the bandits stripped them of their watches, chains, and money; it must have been a very surrealistic scene indeed. "If you see the Pinkertons, tell them to come and get us," they shouted before they left the train.

It seemed that a life of thievery would continue without end for the brothers, especially since they were in the public's favor. Jesse James was a myth among the common folk. Although he had a few setbacks—attacking targets that, in the end, did not reward him with the amounts he expected—he had robbed banks, trains, and coaches with impunity and had escaped from bullets and ruthless detectives. And Jesse had played these games while feeling like a celebrity—one of Jesse's victims even thanked him for distinguishing them with the honor of being assaulted by the famous robber himself. On top of everything, Jesse could read his exploits in the papers as if they were an adventure novel by Karl May. But attitudes were changing, and in the unimportant town of Northfield, the tables started to turn against the gang. It seemed as if Jesse's immense reserves of luck had been depleted.

Northfield was a peaceful and orderly farming community with a single bank, where the savings of the hard-working mill town of 2,000 inhabitants were kept. Jesse expected to secure one of the biggest heists of his career, close to $75,000. It was September 1876, and the money from the freshly harvested crops would be in the vault. Not everyone in the gang agreed. Some were beginning to yearn for a quiet life with their girlfriends, who would hopefully become their wives, and to dedicate themselves to raising cattle.

Perhaps the comrades of the James brothers agreed to this one last job before reforming their lives. The plan took several weeks to materialize. The band traveled to Minnesota separately, meeting in agreed-upon towns, spending days in hotels, drinking and playing poker, and then moving on. Closer to Northfield, they bought horses and trained them to learn not to fear the noise of gunfire. Meanwhile, the bandits began making separate peaceful raids into Northfield, wearing their long coats, with their guns hidden under their linen dusters. They studied escape routes, searched for hiding places, and talked to the inhabitants, pretending to be ranchers interested in purchasing a piece of land. Come the day, they would be stationed in three different places: three on the edge of the town, two outside First National Bank, and three would commit the robbery. In case of trouble, the three men guarding outside Northfield would gallop in and fire their pistols to scare people off. After the break-in, they would meet in the town of Rochester, where they would separate again and return to the safety of Missouri. Nothing could go wrong.

At two o'clock in the afternoon, Jesse and two accomplices approached the bank. They dismounted to have breakfast peacefully—ham and four eggs each—at J. G. Jeft's Restaurant, where they chatted with the owner like any other patron. They immediately went to the bank, while the other group, consisting of two bandits, took up their positions in front of the building. When Jesse and the other man stepped inside, the accomplices locked the door and stood guard. But after this point, the plan began to fall apart.

The owner of the town's hardware store tried to enter the bank to do some business, but one of the bandits stopped him and told him to go away. A few steps away, a young medical student named Henry Wheeler, who was in the town on vacation, witnessed this suspicious interaction and ran to the bank, but he stopped at the sight of a huge revolver between his eyes.

Undaunted, he ran back to get a gun and climbed to the upper floor of a building, from where he began shooting at the robbers. In the meantime, the store owner ran through the street, screaming, "Get your guns, they're robbing the bank!" The two outlaws started to fire their pistols in the air to intimidate the people, but it looked as if the entire town had been waiting for such an occasion to use their guns. After all, it was hunting season. The inhabitants of Northfield rushed for their arms and began to pull their triggers at First National Bank, while the two desperate bandits awaited the help of those on the outskirts of town. Sure enough, when they heard the gunfire, they hastily rode from their positions to help their comrades get out of there. The church bells rang. Even the girls from the nearby Carleton College each took an ax, ready to put up a fight if necessary. Some inhabitants threw stones. The men of Jesse's band started to drop dead or fell from the injuries they sustained under the heavy fire.

But what was happening inside the bank? The men inside were meeting their own nightmare, as they had been obstructed with fierce resistance. After they drew their revolvers from under their clothes and demanded to see the vault, the cashier tried to trap one robber inside. The teller had run from his chair and closed the heavy door, but he failed and was punished for his actions. Still resisting, the brave bank employee refused to open the safe, falsely claiming that it had a time lock. He held firm to this, even though he had a gun on his temple and a superficial cut in his throat. Another clerk, surnamed Bunker, ran to the rear exit and into the alley. One of the bandits shot him but missed hitting his vital organs. The young man reached the street, screaming for help, while Jesse and his two companions heard their desperate partners urging them out. "Better get out, boys, they're killing us!" Furious, Jesse James ran over to the cashier, who was lying helplessly on the floor. He must have thought it was all over, that the men had given up. Sadly, it was over for him as well, for Jesse shot him in the head.

Outside, Jesse saw that the street had become a battleground. The bandits were shooting from behind some wooden boxes, but they were being battered by the people of Northfield. One of the gang members, Stiles, lay dead. Frank had been hit in the leg, and the elbow of one of the Younger brothers had been shattered by a gunshot. The bank robbers fled toward the river, through streets littered with broken window glass, as they dodged the bullets. Cole Younger bravely returned to pick up his brother, who was lying on the ground, and he galloped after his cronies, who were heading toward the Cannon River. But it had not ended. The bold inhabitants of Northfield rushed to their horses to pursue the gang and, hopefully, bring it to an end once and for all. In their haste to flee, the six surviving members forgot to cut the telegraph lines, and soon the entire region was alerted, unleashing the most intense manhunt ever known in the state and even the country. And the gang had only taken $26.60 from the bank. The following days would be the most challenging for Jesse James and his men, as they were wounded and unable to seek refuge.

A Narrow Escape

Battered, wounded, and with two partners dead, the gang wandered the countryside for days, mostly on foot, under cold, eternal rain. Jesse wanted to leave the wounded because of the blood trail they were leaving and the fact they were slowing the others down. Jesse knew that by carrying the wounded with them, they had a higher risk of being captured by the great manhunt that had been organized after the Northfield fiasco. It was probably for this reason that a bitter argument broke out among the members of the band. In the end, they decided to separate and form two groups. Jesse and Frank stuck together, while the rest went the other way. This proved to be a stroke of luck for the James brothers. When the Younger brothers and their posse stopped at a farm to ask for lodging, they were recognized by the farmer's son, who rode eight miles to Madelia to inform the inhabitants that the famous outlaws were at his house.

After an intense shooting, in which one of the bank robbers was killed, the Younger brothers were captured and arrested. They were practically dead themselves. One of them had eleven gunshot wounds in his body. In the meantime, Jesse and Frank James were desperately crossing hostile territory, heading for Dakota. They avoided any human being, stole food from the fields to survive, and made it through the harsh autumn weather. But they survived. "In every way," one of their pursuers later remembered, "they were masters of the situation. Their bravery and their endurance on horseback for days and nights, wounded and almost starving, and without sleep, are without parallel in the history of crime." They made it to Kentucky and then to Texas, where they crossed the border to spend some months in Mexico. This time in their lives is mysterious, as little is known, meaning legend is interwoven with history.

In Old Mexico

In a town near Matamoros, on the border between the US and Mexico, the town's holiday was being celebrated. There was a very crowded dance when two dirty, bearded Americans suddenly entered, dusty after several days of riding. The reigning happy mood seemed to infect them, and they decided to participate in the festivity and asked a couple of Mexican girls to dance.

Amused, the young women accepted the invitation, trying not to laugh as they turned their faces away so as not to smell the unpleasant odor of the strangers and avoided their clumsy dance steps. Little by little, the girls' giggles grew louder until the whole party erupted into a torrent of laughter at the sight of the inept dancers. Infuriated, one of the Americans punched one of the unkind Mexicans, while his partner drew his pistol to kill another. There was then a devilish confusion that the strangers took advantage of to flee, leaving five dead and several wounded on the dance floor. Jesse and Frank James, the legendary American gunmen, had staged the first of a long series of bloody episodes in Mexico.

Toward the beginning of 1877, the brothers appeared in the north of the state of Chihuahua, near a mining town. They had settled in a ranch and won the confidence of the people. One morning in May, six packs of mules passed by, carrying seventy-five kilos of silver bars each, guarded by a detachment of eighteen men with pistols. Jesse, Frank, and three criminals who had joined them asked the muleteers to let them accompany them since the route to Chihuahua was infested with hostile Native Americans. The chief of the muleteers agreed, thinking that the journey would be safer if his group was more numerous.

On the fifth day, the caravan, exhausted from fatigue, fell asleep. Only two remained on guard. The James brothers and their gang treacherously murdered them silently. Then they disarmed the rest of the muleteers and tied them to some trees.

In Piedras Negras, Coahuila, they were assaulted by a band of Mexican bandits. In the resulting shooting, Jesse suffered a wound to his arm. The James brothers then rode to Monclova, where they met a former bandit who had once worked with them in William C. Quantrill's gang. This former gang member had become a respectable businessman, and he was married to a Mexican woman. To celebrate their reunion, the old marauder threw a party at his house.

Between drinks, Jesse noticed that a lieutenant in the Mexican Army was staring at him. He discussed the matter with his brother, but Frank did not care. Soon after that, Jesse saw that his concerns were not unfounded. Peering out a window, he saw a group of soldiers surrounding the house. Suddenly, the besiegers slammed down the doors, and the officer ordered the James brothers to surrender.

"Let the women out first, and we'll fix it," Jesse suggested. The lieutenant accepted. He ordered the women to leave and announced, "There is no possibility of escape. Surrender your guns." But the James brothers fired back. They jumped out of a window, and under cover of darkness, they managed to escape back to Texas, where, according to legend, they served as vigilantes and liquidated a Mexican bandit named Bustendo, who was ravaging the region.

Chapter Five – A Man Named "Howard"

"They continued the war after the war ended; such, at first, was their declared purpose, and, in a measure, so executed. But as time passed on the war, even to them, was a thing of the past, but having imbued their natures in crime, they became the outlaws they now are."

—*Kansas City Times*, July 27th, 1881

Like a wounded beast, Jesse James remained out of the public eye for two years after Northfield, hoping that as time went by, the pressure would lessen and possibly erase the memory of his last failure, which had almost cost him his life and had effectively marked the end of his band. For years, Jesse lived incognito with his family, near Nashville, under another name: John Davis Howard. In 1878, his wife had twins, but they died shortly after birth. Although he posed as an honest farmer, whose passion seemed to be only horses and playing cards in his spare time, Jesse was constantly on the alert. One of his horses was saddled all the time; he carried revolvers and slept with a gun under his pillow. In contrast, his more refined brother Frank, who also lived incognito, seemed to be enjoying his new life. He made friends with his neighbors, attended church, and met up with his acquaintances to talk about Shakespeare. Frank even befriended the Nashville cops, while thirty-two-year-old Jesse languished and died of boredom.

Apparently, his career was over, but he was still restless. Legend says that during his last months as a "family man," he visited Las Vegas and met Billy the Kid. Supposedly, the two famous outlaws discussed the possibility of joining forces. However, according to Jesse's biographer T. J. Stiles, this is "a very questionable account.". In 1879, Jesse finally gathered people to form a new gang. But there was an important difference. This was no brotherly band made of ex-guerrillas and idealist fighters. The recruits were much younger, greedier, and harder to handle. Among them was a new pair of brothers, Robert (better known as Bob) and Charles (better known as Charley) Ford. But at least they decided to follow Jesse into this new chapter of his life, one that would be very short. Jesse stopped a train in Glendale, Missouri, and robbed the passengers with these words to the train messenger: "I didn't get your name, but mine is Jesse James." He was back, and he wanted everybody to know it.

However, things had changed. There was no sympathy in any newspaper after the robbery. There was no symbolism other than money-hungry bandits looking to score. There weren't even large amounts of money or gold in the wagons, which was a symbol of the new times when the country's banking system was consolidating—it was no longer necessary to physically transport bills and coins. The Civil War was beginning to become a distant memory in the minds of many people in and around Missouri, and there was no longer the same ardor for the "Lost Cause." Now James's assaults were no longer seen as those of an avenger against the greedy capitalists of the North but as the misdeeds of a dangerous criminal, one who was driving investment away from Missouri, thereby condemning its inhabitants to live in "the Outlaw's Paradise," as a newspaper of Chicago called it. The Democratic nominee in the 1880 campaign for governor, Thomas T. Crittenden, had personally battled guerrillas during the war. He based his campaign by promising the capture of Jesse James, and he even got the railroad companies to offer a reward of $10,000 for the outlaw, dead or alive, plus $10,000 for Frank James and lesser amounts for each one of his henchmen. Several bounty hunters claimed to have killed Jesse James, and many newspapers printed the news about his death, only to later retract it.

Jesse James, possibly the most wanted man alive at the moment, was guilty of overconfidence. Undaunted, he continued to plan new blows. Since they did not know what he looked like, he taunted his pursuers by approaching them in the street and then sending them notes telling them how and where he had seen them. He constantly changed his address, moving from Kentucky to Kansas, and then back to Missouri, where he settled in the town of St. Joseph, committing petty crimes: a coach of passengers, a store, a solitary horseman, and the payroll of a crew of workers, where, for one last time, Jesse showed his legendary Robin-Hood persona. When they robbed the month's payroll of an engineering crowd in Alabama, the bandit returned the money that belonged to the chief of the crew. "The robber inquired if the money was government money or my own money," the man later recalled. "I told them it was mine, meaning that it would form a part of my salary. The robber told me, he did not want it, neither did they take my watch. They said, they only wanted government money."

A year before his death, Jesse carried out his last big hit, one that wiped out what little popularity he had left. During a new train robbery, Jesse unintentionally killed the driver. He had been shooting at the roof of the wagons to intimidate the passengers, but a bullet hit the driver, who, it was learned later, had also been in charge of the train that took the Pinkertons to his farm the night his mother lost her arm and his half-brother died. Witnesses to the robbery agreed that the driver's death had been accidental, but the newspapers were quick to say that the bandit had murdered him in revenge. The search for Jesse James intensified on all fronts, and the pressure mounted. That his head had a price of $10,000, which was offered by the railroad companies, his old enemy, made Jesse furious, but at the same time, he was pleased to be back in the spotlight. He decided to try it one more time, not knowing it would be his last. Or maybe he did know. For the night of September 7th, 1881, Jesse James acted as if he knew it would be the last time.

After stopping the train by piling rocks on the track, Jesse's men boarded the cars, with their guns in the air, and began to strip the terrified passengers of their belongings. But Jesse seemed more eager to be remembered than to get money. When one of the drivers gave him a 50-cent coin, saying it was all he had, Jesse returned it with an extra dollar and said, "This is the principal and interest on your money." When a woman fainted, he wet her face with his handkerchief and gave her a dollar too. He quoted the Bible several times and said that since they were already wicked, they might as well be good at it. He shook hands with some passengers and introduced himself, saying, "Hello, my name is Jesse James." To the engineer, he handed two dollars and told him, "You're a good one; take this and spend it with the boys." Then, he said goodbye to the passengers before leaving the train and claiming prophetically, "This is the last time you will ever see Jesse James."

Death

"Well it was Robert Ford,

that dirty little coward.

I wonder now how he feels,

for he ate of Jesse's bread

and he slept in Jesse's bed,

and he laid poor Jesse in his grave."

–*Jesse James*, author unknown

In the end, Governor Crittenden's plan worked. He believed Jesse's gang was now more about money and less about politics and revenge, so the temptation of an easy win could be the means of winning over one of the younger members of the gang. Ironically, it was the Ford brothers, whom Jesse trusted the most, who fell for the easy win and especially for the fame they would gain by bringing about the demise of a great legend. Bob Ford, who was only twenty at the time, contacted the authorities in Kansas City to speak with Crittenden.

Meanwhile, Jesse told the brothers he had a new job, and to plan the details, they moved into Jesse's house in St. Joseph. The robbery would take place on April 4th, 1882, in Platte City, Missouri. Bob and Charley were getting more and more nervous living in the house of the bandit they planned to kill. Jesse was quick with the gun, and any mistake would only spell a horrible death for the Fords. They would have to surprise him while he was unarmed, an impossible situation. But the opportunity came on the morning of April 3rd, after breakfast.

According to the Ford brothers, Jesse's wife was in the kitchen, the children were playing outside, and the notorious outlaw went to a painting on the wall to straighten or dust it off. Unusually for him, he took off his guns for a moment to climb onto a chair and move the painting. He placed his revolvers on a bed. Why he took his guns off has intrigued historians. It was unusual for him to lay down his guard for even a second, much less in the company of other men who could betray him. "He was so watchful that no man could get the drop on him," as his killer would go on to say later. Perhaps Jesse trusted the Ford brothers, or maybe he was trying to show them that he still trusted them so they would become easy targets after the next robbery. We can only speculate.

Bob Ford, who was standing behind Jesse, knew this was his chance. Approaching from behind, he drew his revolver and made a little click as he hammered his gun. Jesse began to turn around to see what was going on. Then Bob shot him in the head, and the most famous American bandit of all time fell to the floor, bleeding badly from his head. He was dying. His wife heard the gunshot from the kitchen and ran to see the scene. Crying, Zee desperately tried to stop the bleeding, but it was too late. Jesse died in her arms.

The brothers ran in fear, shocked by the magnitude of what they had done. From the modest house, they rushed to the telegraph office to send a statement to Governor Crittenden: I HAVE KILLED JESSE JAMES.

The news spread like burning powder. Within minutes, the James home in St. Joseph was packed with onlookers who had heard the incredible news. Here lay the man who had lived among them under a false name, the man they now knew was none other than Jesse James. Zee, his tearful wife, revealed his identity to the lawmen. His beard was dyed black, and he was less skinny than in his youth, but he was indeed the famous wanted man. This was confirmed more than a century later with a DNA test when his remains were exhumed in 1995, but well into the 20th century, many impersonators stepped forward, claiming to be Jesse James.

Frank James heard the sad news, but he did not attend the funeral for fear of arrest. For most of Missouri, it was good news. Months later, Frank turned himself in to Governor Crittenden, and he was accompanied by his friend, the journalist John Newman Edwards, who negotiated fair treatment with the authorities.

In a mock trial, Jesse James's murderers were sentenced to death by hanging, only to be pardoned by the governor, who then gave them a part of the reward. But history did not treat Bob Ford, the man who hoped to be a hero for killing Jesse James, well. After the bandit's death, the Ford brothers had to go into hiding because they feared being attacked by the public. Soon after, a song appeared about the adventures of the famous outlaw. Its author is unknown, as well as the year of its appearance in oral tradition. Popular lore glorified Jesse, turning him into a sort of Robin Hood, and repudiated his murderer. "Jesse was a man, a friend to the poor, he couldn't see a brother suffer pain, and with his brother Frank he robbed the Springfield bank, and he stopped the Glendale train." The song was performed in the streets, sometimes with different lyrics, according to the taste and creativity of the interpreter, and it was a quick success. Above all, it contributed to the glorification of Jesse James, who had spent more than half his life as an outlaw. It was his revenge on those who had done him wrong.

Conclusion

For a long time, the murderer of Jesse James toured the country reenacting his deed in a popular play, which he always ended with the words "And this is how I killed Jesse James." But after a while, the novelty wore off. Most people, although they recognized that the death of the bank robber had been for the common good, saw Bob as a traitor and a viper. The truth is that Bob and Charley never slept soundly again, and life became intolerable for them. Charley committed suicide two years later, highly depressed after suffering from tuberculosis. Bob, who worked in circuses and Wild West shows, was shot down by a man hoping to be remembered for having shot the man who shot Jesse James. And then Bob Ford's name was forgotten, while the name of his victim, Jesse James, became legendary. Newspapers contacted all the living people who had known the most famous bank robber in the country, and they began to build upon the legend with the sometimes-fanciful material that people contributed. A large number of dime novels and books appeared about Jesse James's life as an outlaw. His brother Frank lived an honorable and quiet life for many years until his death in 1915. He died at the age of seventy-two.

People continued to visit the house where the rebel had died, as well as the farm where Frank and Jesse grew up. There, a mother in financial hardship received tourists and charged them a small fee for the tour, plus a little extra if the visitors wanted to take a souvenir, such as a sliver from the fence or a pebble from the ground. The visitors saw the places where Jesse and Frank had played, worked, slept, and been nursed by their mother, who never made apologies for her sons. "No mother ever had better sons," she used to say. This was the same woman who wrote a powerful epitaph for Jesse, who, sure enough, had been a ruthless, merciless executioner but also a symptom of social unrest. He was a so-called "social bandit," who represented the voice of the voiceless. He rests forever in Mount Olivet Cemetery, Missouri, under this epitaph:

In Loving Remembrance of My Beloved Son, Jesse W. James.

Died April 3, 1882.

Aged 34 Years, 6 Months, 28 Days.

Murdered by a Traitor and a Coward whose Name is Not Worthy to Appear Here.

Here's another book by Captivating History that you might like

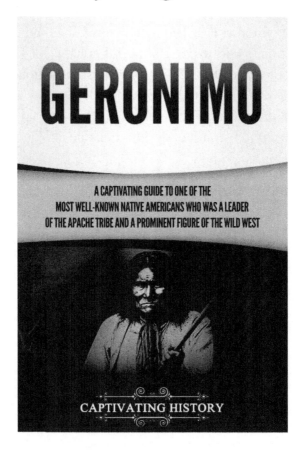

Free Bonus from Captivating History (Available for a Limited time)

Hi History Lovers!

Now you have a chance to join our exclusive history list so you can get your first history ebook for free as well as discounts and a potential to get more history books for free! Simply visit the link below to join.

Captivatinghistory.com/ebook

Also, make sure to follow us on Facebook, Twitter and Youtube by searching for Captivating History.

Bibliography

Edwards, John N. *Noted guerrillas, Or, The warfare of the Border.* St. Louis Missouri: Bryan, Brand & Company, 1877.

Gardner, Mark Lee. *Shot All to Hell: Jesse James, the Northfield Raid, and the Wild West's Greatest Escape.* William Morrow, 2013.

James, Jesse. *Jesse James, My Father.* Kansas City: The Sentinel Printing Co., 1899.

Ortiz T., Manuel. "Jesse James en México". *Contenido* Magazine, March 1970, Mexico, DF.

Smith, Tom. "Jesse James in Iowa." *The Annals of Iowa* 40 (1970), 377-380.

Stiles, TJ. *Jesse James: Last Rebel of the Civil War.* Vintage, 2010.

Woog, Adam. *Jesse James.* Chelsea House Publishers, New York, 2010.

Wukovits, John F., *Jesse James.* Philadelphia: Chelsea House Publishers, 1997.

Printed in Great Britain
by Amazon